HELP ME FIND MY
IDENTITY

HELP ME FIND MY IDENTITY

The Cry of a Young Adult

FAVOUR GAIBO

Contents

Dedication viii
Foreword ix
Preface xi
Introduction xiii

One
The Word of God 1

Two
The BattleField of The Mind 11

Three
Fear Cripples Abilities 24
A Safe Space to Write Down Your Thoughts 35

Four
Value 36

Five
A Letter to Parents 45

Six
The Person of The Holy Spirit 48

Epilogue 54
About The Author 56
References 57

Copyright © 2023 by Favour Gaibo

All rights reserved. No part of this book may be reproduced in any manner whatsoever without written permission except in the case of brief quotations embodied in critical articles and reviews.

First Printing, 2023

I dedicate this book to Mr. and Mrs. Sokeipiriala Gaibo. Thank you for parenting me in the way of Christ and showing me what it means to be Christ-like. I appreciate you both; God bless you.

Foreword

It has been my pleasure and privilege to have known Favour Gaibo since she was a freshman at the University of Prince Edward Island. Since she came to Charlottetown PE and joined the church, I have watched her grow in her relationship with the Man Christ Jesus and transform by becoming confident and embracing the purpose of God over her life.

This well-cultivated, eloquent, and exhilarating work gets to heart the most important subject in the life of young adults in the world where social media has the greatest influence in shaping the lives of many.

Finding your identity is a journey and not a destination, in this book, Favour shares some great insight as the Holy Spirit has taught her and some of her personal journey experience in finding help.

In the Bible the life experience of some prophets became a message to their generation similarly this exceptional work by Favour Gaibo is a message to our generation, this is indispensable reading.

The author's approach to this timely and critical issue brings a fresh breath, captivates the heart, engages the mind and inspires the spirit of the reader.

I highly recommend *"Help Me Find My Identity - The Cry of a Young Adult."* It is definitely Holy Spirit-inspired and full of Wisdom that will stay with you long after you finish reading it.

-Pastor John Cuma

Preface

We can all agree that we came onto this earth without training or knowledge of our left from our right; we had to figure things out ourselves. I believe our different environments and circumstances shape how we view the world, which sometimes eventually forms our character, dreams or what we might call our "identity." For example, someone who struggled for food and other basic needs through the primary stage of life can come off as assertive or be very parsimonious. Alternatively, they can decide never to see anyone else struggle the same way they did and start a foundation. That is just one example, but the point is that our environment, one way or the other, affects us and how we view ourselves. It takes a child from an abusive home to live in a peaceful environment before they can view love from people as something good and not strange. And because most people find themselves in environments they do not choose, they tend to take up a wrong identity. Hence my writing of this book. When you identify who God has made you to be, which is truly who you are, you can pass through the most challenging circumstances in life without allowing that environment to leave its negative aura on you. Knowing who you are (identity) is the foundation for everything in life; once you do, you will not be shaken by anything (Matthew 7:24-27).

Matthew 7:24-27

"Everyone then who hears these words of mine and acts on them will be like a wise man who built his house on the rock. And the rain fell, and the floods and torrent came, and then the winds blew and slammed against that house, yet it did not fall because it had been founded on the rock.

King David in the Bible grew up without love and care, He only had His God, and that was all he needed to know how to love people and know good from evil. His bad environment did not leave a negative aura on him because He knew his identity was in His God.

By the grace of God, this book will guide you on how to build a strong foundation which will eventually help you find your identity.

Introduction

Identity is a sense of who you are as an individual. One prominent thing about identity is that it contributes to one's self-image: that is, how one views himself or herself. Identity affects a lot of our behaviour; it could affect one's posture, tone of voice, abilities, and charisma. Sometimes we refer to people who are not bold as one with low self-esteem, but the truth is that person may not understand their identity. Sometimes people who have not yet understood their identity could be going through depression, anxiety, or what we would call a mental breakdown in our times. Usually, these depressive crises occur more often in ages 14-25 years (APA, 2013; Hewlett & Moran, 2014) when people are just figuring out the world.

People who have found or understood their identity are more optimistic, accomplished, calm, and relaxed.

Identity usually stems from one of the most critical questions, "Who am I?" which usually brings about direction and purpose in life. The answers to this question usually bring a firm conviction in one's faith, personality, dreams, and goals. Your answer can either make or mar you. The earlier you find answers to these questions, the sooner life makes more meaning to you, and the sooner you become purpose-driven, marking out the traits for your legacy.

One

The Word of God

Finding your Identity through the Word of God

The word of God explains the life of Jesus because all you need to have a fulfilled life is Jesus! The Bible, Colossians 3:1-3 tells us that the moment you give your life to Christ, you become a mystery to this world and the people who are in it. Verse 3 says my life is hidden in God, I'm a mystery to this world; if I am living according to Christ, I seem weird to the world. Now the only person that can explain to me who I am is He who owns the life which I have borrowed vs4- "If Christ owns my life, then my identity can only be decoded by the One who owns it-

There is a famous saying that, *"If you do not know the purpose of something, you will misuse it,"* and I add you will not be able

to use it to its maximum potential. You cannot fully utilize a piece of equipment until you have read the maker's manual. I will explain it using a modern-day example. Sometimes because most equipment are similar, that is: the on button all have the same power sign, the handles look alike, the socket plugs almost always resemble each other, we do not read the maker's manual before using the equipment, and we end up losing out on specific features of each item, not utilizing our money. This is the same for us humans. Sometimes we share similar physical characteristics like our hands or eyes or even similar personalities like being an introvert. Nevertheless, in our similarities, we must realize that we have some specific features that we cannot fully comprehend until we return to our maker's manual, which is the word of God.

The word of God is eternal,.In spite of what some humans believe, the word of God was inspired by God to guide men on this earth. The word of God tells us how God's kingdom works and how the world is supposed to function. The word of God shows us how to live our lives and optimize our God-given talent. Some people believe men wrote the word of God, so they do not think highly of everything in it. I would like you to know that the word was written centuries ago by men like Moses, John, Luke and the like, who were all inspired by the Holy Spirit. They had no access to history or computers and study materials, and to prove the word's authenticity, these things written in the word can be traced in history and used to explain the present world. The word of God is perfect and complete; it refers to every possible thing you can think of- 2 Timothy 3:16-17

All Scripture is inspired by God and is useful to teach us what is true and to make us realize what is wrong in our lives. It corrects us when we are wrong and teaches us to do what is right. God uses it to prepare and equip his people to do every good work.

let us look at an example to help you believe that it was genuinely inspired by the Holy Spirit, who is not a human being but God Himself.

In the book of Genesis, the first book of the Bible, God makes the sun, moon and stars and says it is to tell us times and seasons (Genesis 1:14-16). Little wonder that Sumerians, the people who made the calendar, relied on the moon to determine the periods of a calendar (Gary Thomson, 2011). They were among the first to use astronomical observations (study of the sun, moon and stars) for timekeeping. They studied the moon's cycle and said we have 12 months in a year with 365.24 days, making every four years a leap year (a full year of 366 days).

This book, the Bible, has been around for more than 2000 years and will always be there because the word is Jesus Himself (John 1:1) and Jesus can never die. This just means that the word of God displays the life of Jesus. This word is literal, complete, and whatever you need is in it. It is the manual for life. The word of God has characters we could learn from, instructions that should never be altered, prophecies of the earth to be fulfilled, promises for our benefit, and reminders of who God has made us to be. Abiding by the word of God gives you the best life you can ever have, and even when you're in the most excruciating situation, it teaches us how to pray so we can get an overwhelming peace that passeth all understanding (Philippians 4:6-7).

The Bible is also an ancient book with much history that shapes the world's pattern today. It also shows how the earth and systems of the world were made and how God wants the world to run. For example, the first people who made the airplane- the Wrights brothers, had to study one of God's creations, the bird. From that study, a book called Bird's flight was written on the basis of aviation. as the basis of aviation (Otto Lilienthal, 1889). Pilots have to take a bird alleviation course to be able to fly a plane. This is to tell you many things are shaped by how God made them, which can be found in the word of God. So if you are having difficulty with anything in this life, look to the word of God, and you will find answers.

FINDING YOUR IDENTITY THROUGH HIS WORD

The word of God makes us know that we are made in the image and likeness of God according to *Genesis 1:27; "So God created mankind in his image, in the image of God, He created him; male and female He created them."* This means that when we stand in the mirror, we should have *the image and likeness* of Jesus Christ. Simply put, we need to look like Jesus in our minds, character, and every aspect of our lives. We must also believe that we look like Him even physically. The Bible says Jesus grew in physique, wisdom and strength, which means that He created you as beautiful as He looked while on earth. Look in the mirror and always confess the right words;"I am beautiful; I am bold; I am confident."

Moreover, to know what Jesus looked like, *that is*, His ways, His character, and His mind, you need to study the Bible. Fortunately, Jesus came to earth about 2000 years ago, and He exemplified what we should look like, and the Bible records what He did and how He addressed different situations. Studying the Bible will align our characters, our decisions, and our thoughts with that of Jesus.

THE IMAGE OF CHRIST

Speaking about the image, in reading the Bible, you will see you were wonderfully and fearfully made regardless of what form or shape your mirror shows you. (psalms 139:13-14- *For You formed my inward parts; You covered me in my mother's womb. I will praise You, for I am fearfully and wonderfully made; Marvelous are Your works and that my soul knows very well*). That scripture shows that you were made in detail. Do you think the God who created the beautiful birds, the sun, the moon, and all the animals with their different complexities would fall short when making the one He calls His image? What do you see when you look in the mirror? Do you think you are beautiful? Do you find faults with certain parts of your body? Maybe you think your stomach is bigger than it should be, or maybe you prefer to be light skinned? Perhaps, you have a broken arm, came out of the womb with a biological defect, or don't look like what the culturally accepted norm says, God still says in Songs of Songs 4:7 that you are altogether beautiful my darling; and there is no flaw in you. I can tell you that God still made you in His image, and you were created for a purpose. The story of a man born blind in John 9:1-13 lets us know that he did not sin, neither did his parents, but it was so that the name of God will be glorified, and if you think you went through so much pain just so that God's name alone will be glorified, then you need to see how this man's life turned around, and people could not recognize him because God used him for a wonder. He became a star. You also need to see how his story, out of the numerous miracles Jesus performed, made it to the Bible, one of the world's most significant history books. Regardless of our appearance, God made us each uniquely for a purpose. The Bible tells us that He declares the end from the beginning (Isaiah 46:10). He can tell you the end of your life before you even start it. Myles Munroe explains this: God had already finished our lives before He made us start it. This shows us that there is a purpose we need to fulfill and that all we need to thrive in this life has already been provided for us. This is one of the main reasons you should not commit suicide because all you need for life has already been provided. You just need to ask God and study His word while being patient; you shall get it.

Do you struggle with what you see when you look in the mirror? Or you probably have friends whose light skinned faces glow or friends who have started growing beards that make them look more handsome and it seems like everyone sings their praises and you do not get noticed. If you feel this way, here are some steps that would help you overcome that feeling.

- The puberty stage for every human is different and everyone grows at different rates. Regardless of what you see now, everyone is fearfully and wonderfully created by

God. . I remember one of my classmates from high school; he wasn't very tall and was often laughed at because of his height. However, after graduating from University, to everyone's surprise, he grew a lot taller. The way you look today may not be how you would look in 4 years. The society we live in makes us think that there is a certain way to look. And so, unconsciously, women think that they need makeup to look beautiful. Do not get me wrong, I am not against make up, I put makeup on sometimes but there is a problem when you do not love your face the way it is and you feel like you have to cover up some flaws. Some women even go as far as adding silicons to their breasts and butt to make it look bigger. These actions are signs of low self esteem and sometimes, some girls and boys are forced to compare themselves to what they feel is the societal beauty norm. What you should know is that most of the models you see online wear subtle makeup. Most of their pictures are even edited to look flawless. Isn't it unreasonable to want to look like a technologically edited person? Sweetheart, if God says you are beautiful, believe it, because He does not lie! The Bible says that God is not a man that He should lie (Numbers 23:29). So if He says you are beautiful, believe it.

- How you think of yourself is how you will see yourself. In the next chapter of this book, I will be talking about the mind and how your thinking affects what you see. When you confess the right things, you begin to change your mindset which eventually changes what you see in the mirror. So next time you look into the mirror, instead of saying "I am not beautiful enough or my tummy is too big for my body or "I am too dark," say things like, "I am made in God's image." (Genesis 1:27)," I am beautifully and wonderfully made" (Psalms 139:13-14), "I was made for a purpose." (Isaiah 43: 7). "My broken arm or twitchy eyes were made to give God glory." Confess and believe it in your heart and I can promise you that you will begin to see yourself bold and beautiful, the way God sees you.

THE BOLDNESS OF GOD

The likeness of God also refers to His boldness, power, character, and esteem. When Jesus was on earth, He showed boldness. At age twelve, He was at the synagogue answering questions and listening to the scholars teach (Luke 2: 41-47). This likeness, in this case, boldness, has also been given to us. It is written, *"For God has not given us the spirit of fear but of love, power, and sound mind." (2 Timothy 1:7).* This power speaks to both earthly timidity and spiritual fear. You become bold when you know you are far above principalities and powers (dark powers).(Ephesians 1:17-22). This boldness can also be seen when He spoke to the Pharisees. Jesus spoke boldly to these people, and at times, He had to oppose them (mind you, the Pharisees were known to be scholars, and no one dared to oppose them). Jesus also showed boldness when it was time to emit power for healing and deliverance. As scary as delivering a madman may seem, Jesus did it effortlessly without fear and with the help of the Holy Spirit.

I remember reading in the book of Acts where Peter and John were detained and brought to trial by the proconsuls (Acts

4:1-22). The Bible records that the proconsuls knew they were illiterates but listened to them anyway because of their boldness. I had a friend who did not know so much but people always loved to be around her. I always wondered why? Until I came to understand that boldness attracts people. Boldness is like the shiny coating on one's leather shoes. It adds an extra finishing to your charisma. As teenagers, boldness makes you stand up to bullies. Boldness makes people believe you when you speak whether they know you or not like in the case of Peter and John. Peter and John were Christians who prayed for boldness. You will see this right after they were released from the proconsuls trials (Acts 4:23-31).

To be bold, you can simply ask God for it. We can also have boldness by understanding that Jesus has carried all our sins and physical sickness to the cross and greatness comes when there is no guilt of sin (2 Corinthians 3:7-12).

TAKEAWAY NOTES

- "Heaven and earth may pass away, but My word will remain"-God. The word of God is the truth because it is what God says and how God made things. It does not change the truth, even if I believe or accept something else. The Bible says when you know the truth, it will set you free (John 8:32), which means you will forever be in bondage till you know the truth. And the truth can only be found in God's word - PK Olawale.
- In a world where everyone has an opinion, we must

hold on to a standard that has passed the test of time and will not change- The Word of God.
- This is an excellent opportunity for you to accept Jesus's life. All you need to do to start living this new life is to say this prayer:
- Father, I acknowledge that I have sinned by not accepting Your life; I accept that You died on the cross so that I can live again in the fullness of You, I accept this life that you have given to me, and I declare You to be my Lord and personal Saviour.
- If you have said this prayer with me, please join a faith-believing church near you, study the word of God and pray daily to grow your relationship with God.

Two

The BattleField of The Mind

As a person thinks in his heart so is he (Proverbs 23:7)

    The mind is man's most significant asset because that is where he first creates. The mind has no limit to what it can think of. The mind cannot be stopped from exploring ideas. Rich people will always say that becoming rich starts in the mind; you have to think of it before achieving it. Motivational speakers will tell you to consider the goal and see yourself working toward it. Once you can think of it, you can do it.

    Because of how lively the mind is, the devil attacks it, which is why it is a battlefield. Those thoughts of suicide, where does it first happen? in the mind. The hurtful words people say to us are re-spoken in the mind. **A psychological definition of identity is the mental understanding of who you are. This definition means that the origin of identity starts from the mind and the proper mental understanding can only be gotten from the word of God as we have addressed.** For example, God says that you are beautifully and wonderfully made and that you are made in His image as we have seen in chapter one of this book but if someone tells herself that she is not beautiful, standing in front of a mirror or not, her eyes are already programmed not to see beauty. But if she says she is beautiful, and she has been wonderfully made, when she looks into the mirror, she will see nothing less than beautiful. Let me surprise you, the way you appear in your mirror is only in your mind. When you look in the mirror, you might condemn yourself and only see how big your face is or how uneven your skin is. However, someone who has a positive mind can also look at you and see how beautiful you are. It's all in your mind. That's why you must build your mind to accept only what God says about you and not the unrealistic norms the society has created to limit you. God says all He made is good, and all things are created for a purpose. Look in the mirror and confess those positive words daily, and you will start to see them.

Because the mind will grow with what you feed it, you must stay in a positive environment if you can. Stay away from bad vibes, people who do not see you as what God has called you, and those who always speak negatively to you. And if you can't stay away from these people, because of family or restrictions,

the last chapter was written specially for you. I have a friend who can help you.

Now that you know what the word says, walk in that light; carry yourself like you are the most beautiful person, speak like the most fluent person, read like the most intelligent person. Confidence certainly rubs off on people. Your confidence would be so strong that even if people came against your beauty, your newfound knowledge would be bold enough to shun them. The truth is, bullies are also afraid, and what they fear is confidence. Once you are confident in your ability, it's hard for someone else to tell you otherwise. See yourself like that, talk about yourself like that, and I tell you, people will follow you. You set the standard. People only feed you with the confidence you show them. Just like a dog can sense fear, humans can sense confidence. If you ever speak low of yourself, you need to stop it. If you ever look in the mirror and say, "I'm not beautiful," you need to stop it. And I don't care if you have a broken arm or leg because your beauty is not just in how you look. You are beautiful, and that's on period! Have you seen the light being put under a bushel? No, it's not done; since you know you have light in you, put it on the hill, not under a bushel. Be confident! Be bold! And walk in the light which you are.

WAYS TO MAINTAIN A HEALTHY MIND

There are ways you can keep a positive (healthy mind). I will list some of the few things I do that help me but these recommendations require intentionality and consistency. This practice can take a while before it becomes part of you but be assured that it is going to be worth your effort.

- *Take charge of your environment:* Taking charge of your mind is taking charge of your environment; your mind absorbs what's in your environment. Keep your environment clean of every negative aura and negative people (that is: those videos, people or even some social media content that makes you see things negatively), and your mind will be sane. You have to let go of negative thoughts and always think positively. Since your environment influences your mind, you must take charge of it physically, emotionally, and spiritually. Think positively, and use the word of God as a reference point. You are who you think you are, which should be who God says you are. Giving thanks helps me think positively. When I give thanks, I say to myself, God is good, His plans for me are good, and even my mistakes work together for my good because I love Him. (Romans 8:28). So I give Him thanks in the good and bad, it helps me see the good in every situation thereby helping my thoughts be positive.
- *Don't over-criticize yourself:* Don't over-criticize yourself; there is a place for constructive feedback but not that you find fault in everything you do. For example: If you had a class presentation, instead of first saying, "Did I do this thing well?" or "How I did this, was it okay?," you have to tell yourself, "You did great," "It was perfect." Doing this helped me eliminate a double mind and low self-esteem. I began to assure myself before anyone would do it. It is

good first before any feedback. Learn to appreciate yourself before anyone else; every other person's complement should be an addition. The world is filled with people who are ready to downplay your work and not prepared to see your vision with you, hence why you need to appreciate yourself. Look in the mirror, pat yourself on the back and say you've done well. This does not mean you should not improve yourself; oh no! But first, appreciate yourself. And for people who have had traumatic experiences, you must visit your past. Talk with a spiritual leader or a therapist. It would help if you heal so you can free up your mind. Sometimes you might need to confront that trauma.

- *Avoid Pressure:* Another thing that can make you have an unhealthy mind is pressure. Pressure can make your mind busy as you overthink what you need to grow into. That is why everything in life is done with time. Even the Bible says there is time for everything under the sun. There is time for sowing and reaping (Ecclesiastes 3:1-8); you must be patient. It takes time to grow. David was anointed king (1 Samuel 16:13), but he didn't get to sit on the throne till about 15 years later (2 Samuel 5:1-4); Joseph knew he would be great, but nothing happened till 17 years later (Genesis 37- Genesis 41). Pressure will make you shortchange yourself. Pressure might make you lose your integrity for something which has already been assigned to you. Imagine paying for something that was meant to be a gift to you. The process is there to make you wiser in a particular area and pressure can make you not enjoy that process.

When you shortchange it for something else, you lose the vital training you are to get for that assignment.

ANTIDOTES TO PRESSURE

As you grow, you will tend to see your peers doing a lot of things that are not right, and they might also try to influence/pressure you into doing those things like smoking, drinking, and clubbing. They are getting the fame and money you might desire then, but you must learn to hold on to the new identity that Jesus has given you and wait for everything He has deposited in you to come to fulfillment.

And from my little experience on earth, there will always be a form of pressure, if you are not doing some conscious things to overcome those pressures, they might derail you from your good values. In order to keep my values right and keep my mind focused on my God-given goals, here are some things I do to overcome pressure: being contented with what I have, giving thanks always, and being patient.

Contentment and thanksgiving make you grateful for the little. It helps you enjoy the present while you work towards achieving your future goals and ambitions. Patience is a virtue that gives you the strength to wait for the end to be established. So be content with what you have, be thankful to God for where you are and be patient for what is to come.

- *Avoid having a busy mind:* Do you find yourself confused? Do you struggle to focus on one thing at a time? Do you find that you worry a lot or even often get depressed? Then you probably have a busy mind. A busy mind is one that thinks deeply about things or thinks about multiple things simultaneously. Like any good thing, a busy mind can work for your advantage if nurtured or can be a disadvantage if not groomed. A leader with a busy mind makes excellent decisions, as she will be well-informed before making a decision. However, if she has the wrong set of people around her, she might keep hearing all she needs to work, which she already knows without appraisals; she has a busy mind and will only think deeply about her failures. A busy mind is usually the target of the devil, especially if you are having wandering thoughts. You can be in five places at once, have five situations you have created in your mind, and jump from one to another. A busy mind can easily cause depression because there, you have intrusive thoughts, internal pressure, rationalization,, and negative thoughts from negative comments. A busy mind can come from someone who is fearful, who is idle, or who has an extensively busy schedule. In Joyce Meyer's *Battlefield of the Mind*, she talks about controlling your thoughts and not allowing your thoughts to wander. A busy mind can make one proud, envious, jealous, or easily angered. A busy mind can happen to someone who has gone through some abuse or trauma because they have used their mind as an escape room from their present reality, and even when they are out of that trauma, their mind has gotten so used to it that they keep wandering in their mind. You can get out of it if this is you; you can still be normal; you have to be conscious of what you are thinking about and try to be present and not in different places in your mind.

A Calm Mind

We have been speaking about busy minds and I'm sure you are wondering what a healthy, calm mind looks like. I will give this Bible story to explain it to you. There was a man named Elijah in the Bible, he was a very great prophet of God during his time. At that time, the king and his wife were people who constantly sinned against God, making God's children, the Israelites, worship other gods and God was not pleased about this. God always used Elijah to warn the king and his wife about their wrongdoings. One day, the king's wife, Jezebel, threatened to kill Elijah and Elijah ran into depression. At this point, we can say that his mind was busy. Elijah was anxious, overthinking and worrying over the words of Jezebel. Mind you, this same Elijah is someone who had prayed to God and called down fire on more than fifty people. This same Elijah could disappear and appear in times of trouble with the help of God, but a single threat was what took him into depression, asking God to take his life. God had to make Elijah do a forty-day fast, and after that, Elijah went into a cave and spent the night there, then God told him to stand in front of the mountain, *"and a great and strong wind tore into the mountains and broke the rocks in pieces, but the Lord was not in the wind; and after the wind an earthquake, but the Lord was not in the earthquake; and after the earthquake a fire, but the Lord was not in the fire; and after the fire a still small voice." (1 Kings 19:11-13).* As soon as Elijah heard the still small voice, he went out. This story just shows that when you have a busy mind, you will not be able to hear God's voice properly. Fear, anxiety, and worry had taken over the mind of Elijah. He just kept complaining and could not hear God's voice well. Notice that the still small voice was God.

If your mind is busy, you cannot hear a voice that is still and small. So a clear, healthy mind is one that is calm, and positive. It is not anxious, worried, full of complaints, or scattered.

Ways to have a calm mind

One way to calm a busy mind is to carefully know what you are thinking of. You have to be conscious of what you let your mind ponder on. I used to be someone who had many thoughts at once in my mind. I could be thinking of a show, and the next minute I am calculating the measurements needed to bake a cake, and without finishing the calculation, I can switch to a shopping cart, all in my mind within a few minutes. I had to consciously finish a thought in my mind before I entered another thought.

Another way that helped me calm my mind was to finish one project before moving to another. For example, I write books and songs and I also run a baking business. So I write out the projects and set timelines for each of them and I can't move to the next project without finishing the previous project.

You can also calm your mind by taking breaks from social media. It helps maintain a calm state of mind and allows you to live in the present and not in some fantasized world. Unfortunately, social media does not help with a busy mind. This social media also causes some mental pressure to be quickly rich and famous, which does not always happen that way in the real world.

You can also read books on the mind or positive thinking to

help you maintain a healthy mind; I recommend Joyce Meyers's Battlefield of the Mind.

Action Items

There might be things you are not confident about; please write them out on a piece of paper or in your journal and then stand in front of a mirror and confess positive things to yourself.

The Bible says you have the mind of Christ; therefore, think like Christ. So think of those things which you are not so confident about and write out the positive aspect of it then use one of the below scriptures to back it up, and confess this as much as it comes to your mind. For example, if you think your nose is too big, write down "my nose fits my body perfectly for God says in Psalms 139:14 6:4 'I will praise you because I am fearfully and wonderfully made'". If you are always afraid, you can write down this scripture, "I must not fear them for the Lord my God Himself fights for me" (Deuteronomy 3:22).

Here are some scriptures to help you:

Scriptures for Fear

- I do not have the spirit of fear, but I have the spirit of a sound mind, of power and of love- 2 Timothy 1:7
- I must not fear them, for the Lord my God Himself fights for me - Deuteronomy 3:22
- Then the Lord said to me, "Peace be with me: do not fear for I shall not die - Judges 6:23

Scriptures for Anxiety

- I will be anxious for nothing but in everything by prayer and supplication, with thanksgiving I will make my requests known to God and the peace of God which surpasses all understanding, will guard my heart and mind through Christ Jesus- Philippians 4:6
- Therefore God says to me, do not worry about your life, what you will eat; nor about the body, what you will put on, "If then God so clothes the grass, which today is in the field and tomorrow is thrown into the oven, how much more will He clothe me? And I will not seek what I will eat or drink, nor have an anxious mind. For all these things the nations see after, and my father knows that I need these things. But I will seek the kingdom of God, and all these things shall be added to me. I will not be afraid for it is my father's good pleasure to give me the kingdom- Luke 12:22, 28, 29, 30, 32)

Scriptures for Appearance

- God says to me: My love, you are as beautiful/ handsome as Tirzah, lovely as Jerusalem, and as awesome as an army with banners-Songs of Songs 6:4
- How beautiful are my feet in sandals, O prince's daughter! The curves of my thighs like jewels, the work of the hands of a skillful workman- Songs of Songs 7:1
- I will praise You (God) because I am fearfully and wonderfully made- Psalm 139: 14

Scriptures for a Healthy Mind

- You (God) will keep me in perfect peace for my mind is stayed on You because my trust is in You- Isaiah 26:3
- For God has not given me a spirit of fear but of power love and a sound mind 2 Timothy 1:7

Scriptures for Love

- But God demonstrates His own love towards me, in that while I was still a sinner, He died for me-Romans 5:8
- Who shall separate me from the love of Christ, tribulations, distress or famine or nakedness, or peril, or sword? Yet in all these things I am more than conquerors through Him who loved me. For I am persuaded that neither death nor life, nor angels, nor principalities nor powers nor things to come, nor height nor depth, nor any other created thing shall be able to separate me from the love of God which is in Christ Jesus my Lord- Romans 8:35, 37, 38, and 39.

Scripture for Loneliness

- If I ascend into heaven, You are there; If I make my bed in hell, behold You are there. If I take the wings of the morning, and dwell in the uttermost parts of the sea, Even there your hand shall lead me-Psalm 139:8-10

TAKEAWAY NOTES

The mind influences what you see, how you feel and what you eventually say, which is powerful (Proverb 18:21). Angels act on whatever you say. Also, learn to give thanks when things are not going right, or you can't understand something. Giving thanks reduces grumbling and makes you see things in a better way.

A healthy mind produces a healthy life. Remember, you are what you think.

Guard your environment, the things you see, the people around you, the people you listen to, and the places you visit.

Reading books is very important; I can't emphasize that enough. And I'm not talking about novels or fiction stories, but informative books. Books that give you information. Read books based on what you think you lack: for example, if you are trying to learn good habits and drop the bad ones, you can read *Atomic Habits* by James Clear. If you are up to the age of marriage, read marital books; if you find that you are constantly being depressed for absolutely no reason, read books by Joyce Meyer. These kinds of books make you first see that other people have gone through these situations, so you are not alone, and you can learn how they overcame those challenges. We all came into this world knowing nothing, but if you read books from experiences and tested observations of others, your life will be easier. Do read books; make it a habit, two pages a day is not so much, and it will provide enough information to keep you progressing.

Three

Fear Cripples Abilities

Who Are You?

When I began writing this book, the first line that popped up in my mind was "Fear cripples abilities," which was going to be the title of this book until the Holy Spirit made me understand that you will only be fearful if you do not know who you are. This means that if you know who you are and all the riches you have being a child of God, you will not be afraid of anything.

Fear can suffice from many things, such as an absence of confidence or boldness, holding on to past mistakes, traumatic experiences, uncertainties, fear of the future, fear of the unknown, and fear of rejection. All these are descriptions of fear in different words, and there are many definitions of fear, but fear to me, is the lack of understanding of one's identity. To emphasize this, I will write a few different descriptions of fear that will help you see why they all stem from not fully understanding one's identity.

Fear From Past Mistakes: I have come to understand that this life would not be beautiful without our mistakes or the ups and downs it brings to us. Those bumps on the way of life make it enjoyable. Without them, everything will be straightforward and boring. So mistakes provide lessons for us to learn from. Mistakes give us stories to remember and laugh at. Fear makes you think you are your mistakes. It makes you accept the wrongs that have been said about you or the evils you have called yourself. You now begin to unconsciously act like those wrong sayings, limiting the abilities that God has put in you. You failed a course, and you were told you are dumb, and you begin to think and act like a dumb person; you started a business, and it crashed, and you were told you are a failure; you accept it and begin to walk or act like a failure with your head down, posture bent, and many more things you do unconsciously. I'm not saying that a lack of identity causes all posture defects, but a lack of understanding of your identity can cause these defects sometimes. You need first to know what God tells you about those things and what He thinks about you, then speak and act like what God's word says. When you know your identity in Christ, you will know that all things work together for the good of those who love God and are called according to His purpose (Romans 8:28). This means that all your mistakes work together to give you a beautiful story. That way, you think in a new light; by a new light, I mean you feel the way Jesus thinks of you. There is no one without mistakes, absolutely no one in this life, except

Jesus. And there is also no mistake that God cannot fix. God is not surprised by your mistakes; He knew it would happen! He would have probably been shocked if it did not occur. So know that as long as you are alive, you can still breathe; it means you still have hope, and God is out to help you.

I would love to add that you can be more conscious of your mood. You need to come to the point of being happy when an unplanned mistake occurs. When you've done your assignment and know you did everything you could to be good at something, and a mistake occurs, be happy; see it as an opportunity to learn. Not all mistakes are inevitable! Also, after you've learned about something, please do not be too rigid or conscious; add your creativity to it. Sometimes some people do life a certain way that it becomes boring. I believe God put in us different talents; those talents make life beautiful. Having your pattern of doing something different from others makes life attractive. This is what is called authentic. I do this to the point where I tell my friend, "Who makes the rules". with all the unspoken rules governing life that no one makes but we all seem to follow, we are bound to think some things are mistakes when they just seem different. So allow the creativity God put in you to work sometimes and don't call it a mistake!

Uncertainties, Fear of The Future, And Fear of the Unknown: Sometimes in life, we can get trapped in wanting to know everything, knowing what our future will look like, who we will get married to, and what we will grow up to be, But God did not make life that way. He made life one step at a time; the more steps you take, the more precise the picture becomes. We were not made to know everything, including prophets. You can plan, have faith and hope but leave the rest to God. Remember that God is done with your life before He lets you start it. He told Jeremiah in Jeremiah 1:5, and He is also saying to you: *"Before I formed you in the womb I knew you, before you were born, I set you apart..."* So why worry? He has assured us in the scriptures that He will provide everything you need. Philippians 4:6-7 says to *"be anxious for nothing (this includes the future and the unknown), but in everything by prayer and supplication, with thanksgiving, let your request be made known to God."* Matthew 6:25-33 says look at the birds of the air: they neither sow nor reap nor gather into barns, and yet your heavenly Father feeds them. Are you not of more value than they? This scripture tells us that God cares for us more than we would ever care about ourselves, and He is simply saying, let me do the worrying for you; let me bother about that for you; you just relax and be patient.

Fear of Rejection: It is normal to want to be part of a clique or circle. God made us relational beings; he did not make anyone an Island. But because of a lack of identity, one can think lowly of themselves sometimes. Even in an unhealthy environment, one might fear rejection. This is usually the plan of the devil to make people isolate themselves, try to fill up the relational gap with addictions, or even fall under lousy pressures from peers. When you know who you are, and the amount of riches in store for you to succeed on this planet, you will know not to associate yourself with how people treat you. Humans will treat you based on their perception, but it does not change who God has made you to be.

There is a story of a child who asked his mum what his value was. His mum gave him a diamond and asked him to take it to a cobbler, a doctor, a cook, and a jeweller. He took it to the cobbler; the cobbler told him it could go for $20; he took it to the doctor, and the doctor said it could go for $50; he took it to the cook, and the cook said it could go for $30, then he took it to the jeweller who told him the diamond costs a million dollars. That shows you that humans will only treat you how they perceive you. The only person who knows your actual worth is God. He is the one who knows how much talent He put in you. First, you must know who you are in Christ, who God is and the abundant riches He has stored for you. You can only know that through praying and studying His word. After that, you can now pray to God to lead you to people who have the same mind as you. When you know who you are, you will have a higher sense of confidence and know how to be treated. And anything short of that, you learn to excuse yourself. Remember, humans will only treat you how they perceive you, but that does not change who God created you to be!

From these few types of fear, you can see that fear comes from not knowing your identity in Christ Jesus and not knowing how much riches you have in Him. Ephesians 1:18-19 says, *"The eyes of our understanding being enlightened; that you may know what is the hope of His calling, what are the riches of the glory of His inheritance in saints, and what is the exceeding greatness of His power toward us who believe, according to the working of His mighty power which He worked in Christ when He raised Him from the dead and seated Him at His right hand in the heavenly places"* These scriptures give us an assurance that we are settled and safe in Christ Jesus, having all that we need. Fear impedes all the abilities that God has in you so you cannot see and think the way He made you. If you cannot see yourself the way He sees you, you will produce a lower value than expected.

Sometimes, we do not know when we are walking in fear, so we just move with the flow of things, thinking that is how life should be. However, if we observe ourselves carefully, we will be able to denote its operations. I have carefully written out some symptoms of fear, please note that these symptoms do not always mean that one is fearful but with careful observation, you will know when fear is operating.

Symptoms of Fear

- *Overexplaining yourself:* This happens when you explain yourself when it is not necessary. Sometimes this is good and needed, but when you explain yourself out of compulsion almost always, there is a sort of fear in your life. This usually happens when your self-esteem is yet to be built. Your self-esteem can be built by knowing who God says you are. So spend time with His word.
- *Using your Mind as an Escape Room:* This happens when you accelerate your mind to the future instead of living in the present. For example, you always think of when you will finally be free from that abusive relationship. Instead of facing the reality of the relationship and dealing with it towards freedom, you only live in your mind as though you are free. This is dangerous because it causes you to go

into mental illness and leaves you behaving like a child (as someone who's not mature to your current age). It leaves you in wonderland (in your mind, you are everything; superwoman/superman), but in the physical, you're being trampled upon. You can only say your mind to certain people and not to others. For example, your classmate bullies you and every day you think of how you stand up to him and fight him hands down meanwhile in the physical, you have not done anything to stop the situation. To people, you might seem selfish and proud as you might tend to talk a lot about yourself when all you are doing is finding a way to escape from your reality. To overcome this, you have to deal with the situation. For example, if it is a bully who keeps making you feel less of yourself, you should speak up to some authorities like your teachers or your parents. Some cases might be severe such as rape or marital abuse. For such, you need to seek a therapist.

- *Living to Please Others:* You always do things to please other people without considering if it is the right thing to do. This can be a result of peer pressure; when you do not know who you are in Christ, you might want to live your life according to the status quo provided by your friends in order to make them so you can belong. When you begin to live the Christ-like way, you might realize that you no longer fit in with the friends you used to relate with before, because you are now doing things the right way, which is God's way.
- *Constantly Reminiscing on the Past:* When you constantly remember mistakes or the most humiliating thing you

have done in the past, you slowly become afraid to thread some paths. And sometimes that fear might turn into a strong wall in your life. You need to learn to easily let things go. This helped me when I could not let go of some failures and I know it will help you too- God knows you will make mistakes. He doesn't want you to make them willingly, but He knows they will happen. He expects us to make mistakes because we are His "children" but always know that God is bigger than our mistakes. You have to forgive yourself for the past error because the Bible says: Whatever you lose (forgive) is free, and whatever you bind (hold in unforgiveness) is kept in bondage (Matthew 18:18-20), and this includes yourself. So forgive yourself and move on, for God is a merciful God. And if anyone tries to remind you of your past, be bold and tell them that they're living your past and need to catch up with you as you have moved on.

- *Self-Consciousness:* When you reminisce a lot about the past, you become too self-conscious which can result in you criticizing everything, from your body to your hair to your writing. Being too self-conscious can also disturb your relationship with other people as you soon become a perfectionist. This can be a symptom of fear., You want to make sure that you have freed your mind from the past and that you are taking steps to move on.
- *Overthinking:* Overthinking just like any other thing, can be to your advantage and if not used properly, can also be to your disadvantage. Entrepreneurs and leaders tend to think a lot, that is usually what helps them to grow but

you need to know when to stop thinking, if not, you will create fears that do not even exist. There is a thin line between critical thinking which is what entrepreneurs do, and overthinking. When you begin to think of things that you do not have control over, you have gone beyond critical thinking and you are now overthinking.
- *Negative Thoughts:* As a child of God, you cannot continuously think negatively. It is a sign that you are living in fear. God told us in His word to think of what is pure, honest, just, lovely, and whatever is of a good report (Philippians 4:8). Cultivate a positive mentality and always think on the positive.
- *Body Amendment:* Some people become transgender not only because of how they feel but also because of fear; fear of sexual abuse, and fear of not appreciating their body type (plus size or slim). Instead of facing these fundamental issues, they would become transgender. Running away from problems will only cause a heap; it doesn't solve anything.
- *Lack of confidence:* Lack of confidence can come as a form of stage fright, and the inability to speak up for yourself. I want to tell you today that you can do anything; act confident and bold even when you need help figuring out what to do. Have you ever wondered why a dog would chase you once you start running? It's because they've sensed fear. Same with any other animal or human. People can sense fear, and you don't want that. Because when they sense that fear, they won't stop taking advantage of you. Once

you understand who you are and see yourself the way God sees you, people will be forced to see what you see.

Action Items

- Write out all the behaviours and characters you have that you think are similar to fear.
- After writing them out, prayerfully think of how those fearful behaviours came about. It could be from a childhood trauma a mistake you made in the past or something someone did to you that you did not like and you have not been able to let go of.
- Begin to address them one after the other. Speak to the persons who might have hurt you. Ask questions or see a Christian therapist if you need to. Ask God to help you forgive yourself, and help you heal.
- Now forget the past and move on! *"For whom the son sets free, is free indeed."* (John 8:36)

TAKEAWAY NOTES

You won't be able to live out God's purpose for your life or even live life to the fullest because of the canopy of fear covering you. Fear of what people will say, fear of failing or fear of people. You'll need to remove that canopy to enjoy life. God wants us to enjoy life on earth. He says in Ecclesiastes that it is good for a man to work and eat the fruit of His labour.

Life is step by step; you won't know everything about your life in one day; it comes in bits, even prophecies. It does not always come at once but in bits. So take life a step at a time, don't be anxious about your tomorrow, learn to plan for the future but leave it to God to guide and establish you.

Our identity is what God calls us, not what we call ourselves or what someone else calls or has called us.

Don't be ashamed of what you should be proud of, which is who God has made you to be: your figure, your eyes, your gender, your playful personality. Be happy and content and proud of who you are.

A Safe Space to Write Down Your Thoughts

Four

Value

The Greatest Currency

Proverbs 22:29 Do you see a man who excels in his work? He will stand before Kings; He will not stand before unknown men

One of God's attributes is His creative nature. This same nature was bestowed upon us because we are made in His image (Genesis 1:27). This creative ability He gave to us can be further explained in Exodus 31:1-6 where God said He had given Bezalel, and Oholiab and all the skilled workers the wisdom, skill and ability they needed to do the artistic designs. And we can also see through the scriptures how God has invested one skill or ability in every person. For example, David was skillful in the instrument that brought him close to the throne (1 Samuel 16:16).

Exodus 35:25 talks of the women who were skilled in making scarlet material and fine linen. Another example is Dorcas, also known as Tabitha, who was skillful in making robes. These are all just examples of people who had skills in the Bible. Others were given some abilities: Samson is a perfect example. God gave him strength to fight battles; David was another fellow who was strengthened for battle. Some were trained to be leaders, like Josiah and Deborah.

In this life, God is aware of the need to work and earn money for survival; he has given us skills, passions, and abilities to thrive. A saying goes this way: *"No food for a lazy man,"* which is true. The Bible says: a little slumber, a little folding of hands, and poverty will come. (Proverbs 6:10-11). You might think you are too little to start using your skills, but the youngest billionaire today (August 11th, 2022), Alexandr Wang, is just twenty-five. From a young age, he began to develop his skills; now, his company uses artificial intelligence to analyze how much damage Russian bombs cause in Ukraine.

These skills and abilities can be turned into value and used to provide solutions for humankind on this earth.

THE IMPORTANCE OF ADDING VALUE

Although value is not your identity, it is essential you have it. The whole purpose of this book is to help people find themselves and reduce the number of suicides and depression. If we don't talk about giving value through your identity, people will be depressed as they believe nothing is working for them. This is why this subtopic is vital. You can know who you are in Christ, but if you can't use it on this earth, then it is not complete. I'll always say spiritual things are the most important, but they are raw materials. You won't be relevant on earth if you can't turn it into finished goods that the world can see and understand. In as much as value (what you have isn't your identity, you need it to be able to make respectable transactions with it on earth. I'll explain: have you ever gone to the market without money? You won't be able to take anything home with you. If a wealthy man needs to buy something, the business owner will not say because he is rich, he'll give it for free; instead, he might even charge more. It's the same as the value we carry. Value is the earth's currency. People will listen to what you have to say when you have value. Different countries use different currencies, but the standard money, which can take you to other countries without changing it, is value. Value is the only thing that will never drop with a country's economy. That's why nations can borrow from a person. Imagine that.

Now what is the value? Value is the worth that is being attached to a person. It is something that provides solutions for people which in return, makes these people respect you. Value can be a skill you continuously hone. Value is the investment you have put in yourself. The same way the books you buy on your Apple phone cannot be shared with someone else is the same way your value cannot be shared with another person; they have to earn theirs.

Self-investment involves you taking care of yourself, reading books, investing in a business, investing in education, and the labour of your hands. Adding value will make you stand out. The world not only celebrates beauty but also brains, investments, and solution-givers. Even in fashion shows, they don't only seek beauty; they also seek people who are learned, and so the pageants are also tested in their knowledge. Read books, take extra courses, find a skill to learn, and watch educational and etiquette videos, because you do not know where you will find yourself someday, requiring this acquired knowledge or skill. I heard the story of a woman who had a lot of degrees, even a Ph.D. but could not find a job but then learnt to bake. She now has a big bakery which provides her with millions. Imagine if she did not acquire a skill; she would have to contend with poverty.

Value is relatively easy to get. Value is being diligent in whatever you find yourself in. Be it your academics or a skillful job such as fashion, baking, or graphic designing. Or that thing God has shown you in a dream or spoken to you about. And as long as you have passion for it and are consistent with it, it will go well. And these days, you can get wealthy by being diligent; wealth is far more than just doctors, lawyers or IT students. Just be active and consistent, and you will get to the top.

That talent you think is little might save the day or give the world a new look. So don't let fear stop you; get it!

The Bible also says to whom more is given, more is expected —the parable of the businessman that gave talents to his servants (Matthew 25:14-30). The one given five talents returned with 5, not three, not two. He lived up to what was expected of him. It was the same for the guy with two skills. The guy who was given one and buried it is our focus. He lived below what was expected of him, not producing value and, therefore, unproductive in the hand of God. Whenever we do not give importance to what God has put in our hands, we are hopeless in the hands of God. You are not living up to your optimum capacity whenever you produce below what is expected of you. And in most companies, you get fired when the latter happens.

I will also use the fig tree as an example: Jesus was angry with that tree because it was full of leaves, and this shows that it was time to bear fruit. But when Jesus looked, there was no fruit. Many of us are like that tree; we look like we should be bearing fruit, but when checked, we are not giving any value, producing any worth, or even making an impact. I was once like that. I always wondered why I was picked on when I wasn't the only one who failed a subject or a test; I always wondered why I got laughed at the most when others didn't do well. Then the Holy Spirit made me realize that I looked like a fig tree, having lots of leaves but not bearing any fruits. Unknown to you, men can see when you have potential, but you disappoint them when you don't produce any fruit. Have you ever anticipated a really hyped movie, but after you watched it, you were disappointed? This is more like when your vocabulary, dressing, and mannerisms show potential, but you're not using it by producing fruits. You want to add value so that your looks match what you have inside.

I would like you to know that men will always seek value. When people go to business meetings or non-business conferences, people are either selling themselves or professionals are looking for friends who have value and can benefit from their lives one way or the other. You will reach a particular stage when you realize that friendship is about the value someone adds to you, not just about how nice a person is, but how they make you grow. It'll be wise for you to start gaining skills now and begin to do things that add value to you and the people around you, that way you are not in a rush to gain head in public, but with ease, you can gain dominance in your field of study or area of expertise. Usually, youths want things to become big quickly, but when that happens, most times, it is either fraudulent or won't last long. See, life was created to be in stages. You start with baby steps, do a little at a time, and soon you'll realize that you've created an ocean. But keep adding something to your life, and never be idle. Adding value is often solving a problem which adds respect to your name. This could be a skill you learn, knowledge or wisdom you have gained through life experiences.

Value will save you the stress of having to introduce yourself. There is a video with Elon Musk saying, "I don't have to introduce myself, but if you don't know me, my name is Elon Musk." He ends there and says some other things without explaining what Elon Musk does or why he's famous. That's to show you what value does. Value gives you respect and brings you before kings. Value gives you credibility and gives you a voice. You will speak, and people will listen; you will correct, and they will obey, but without value, people will disregard you. Value brings you before kings and gives you an upper hand in society before men (The Bible tells us in Proverbs 22:29, that a man diligent in his works will stand before kings and not mean men).

Take, for example, imagine Elon Musk with another non-famous person arguing about business Elon Musk spills factless points, and that other person spills facts that are backed up by science. The truth is that 90% of the world will accept whatever Elon says, and that's because he has built some credibility in the hearts of men. The worth of Elon Musk is in people's hearts, and even if what he says is inaccurate, his wealth still does not reduce. Our worth (values) brings us before kings; imagine being a Christian who wants to dominate places; without value, you can't convince anybody about Christ. Your worth (value) provides you with the attention of men even if you don't ask for it.

Value gives you influence amongst men. In this end time, the result of our values will make the government stop things like Pride Month. The impact of our values will convince men that your God is great; your influence will make God's government rule on earth. The value Dr.Myles Munroe added made him prominent among governors and leaders even though he was a pastor. These people of high esteem regard his words highly. He spoke the truth about the word of God without fear..

Acts 5:13-14 gives a little understanding of what value does and how it makes people highly esteem you. I was praying one day, and I said that if Christianity were like the time of Peter and Paul, we would have more respect from unbelievers, like in Acts 5. In earlier times, when you think of Christians, you think of long skirts, hair rough-looking, and sometimes even people with body odour. You think of people who are dull and only know how to speak in tongues. And that's why a lot of unbelievers play with Christians. You see a lot in movies where senior pastors 'are sleeping with people or people are joking about sacred things like speaking in tongues. Previously, Christianity was all about praying and dressing. People did evil in their hearts, and that's why Christianity has been dragged in the mud a lot. Thank God for the rising era where a lot has changed, and Christians are now at the forefront of the marketplace, music, and politics.

It's refreshing to see people who are solid about their belief in God doing outstanding things in these secular places; it gives respect to Christians, which is the whole purpose of value. As I said earlier, it provides another level of accountability and credibility.

After reading this scripture in Acts 5, I understand that the world is waiting for my manifestation. Fellow Christians, I say to you; unbelievers are waiting for your manifestation. Working on my purpose adds beauty and colour to life and brings respect to anything I represent. So stand up and add value, do things and make a difference.

As crucial as value is, whatever you have should never replace your identity in Christ. Life happens, and you might lose that value or find out that it's not working as it used to before because when life happens, it can affect the value you've created. For example, you're a footballer who was famous for goals and now in 3 years has a broken leg and can't play anymore; if the playing of football were your identity, you would crumble with it. You can go into depression and sometimes suicide, and you don't want that to happen. Balance is the key here, but you must first know your identity is in Jesus Christ.

With value, you have to do it progressively. It can become outdated. As much as the word value stays the same as money currency does, the world progresses in how things are done. The people who created the first computers, although are on record for their outstanding achievements, their computers are no longer useful. Therefore as long as you are alive, you must always seek to update your value, learn each day, grow your skills, read books! and take courses. Don't relax because you think you've made a name for yourself. In this technology world, things are rapidly changing, and you want to be constantly relevant.

TAKEAWAY NOTES

Myles Munroe once said: People will change their perspective towards you when they know why you're here and when they begin to understand your purpose (*Understanding the Purpose and Power of a Woman*, page 69).

Value gives you an advantage; it covers a lot of mistakes about you. The respect it provides you covers a lot of your mistakes. People see you, and instead of seeing that mistake you can't correct, they see your advantage- Value

Five

A Letter to Parents

Train up a child in the way he should go, and when he is old he will not depart from it- (Proverbs 22:6)

I might not be a parent yet, but one recurring thing I have seen with leadership, nurturing, marriage or anything that involves relationships is that patience is a huge factor. It takes work to change and teach someone new things. Although you have to bear some of the consequences of your children's mistakes, you have to show love for you to get someone to be where you are. If someone keeps shouting at you, whether it is your boss at work or your husband, you will feel unloved even if you see why they shout. You will not take their correction because anything they do will come as hatred to you. It's the same for them; the key is balance. Make sure you show them enough affection while still telling them the truth. It can be likened to telling a 2-year-old who holds a red bowl that the bowl is red, but the child says it's pink. It'll take a few years before they can differentiate between red and pink. What you do in those few years before they can distinguish colours is what matters. I'm not saying butter them up, but please deal with them in understanding, which requires a lot of patience. Sometimes let them make their mistakes and be there to encourage them to rise. Understanding with patience is sometimes letting them do what they want even when you know they'll fail and being there to pick them up when they've fallen.

It'll get to a certain age where you can only advise and not tell them what to do. Please advise and remember, any human would rather listen to someone who has always been there to encourage them than one who is always shouting.

You train your children for the future, literally. So if you make them read for 2 hours daily, you start an intelligent habit with them. The Bible says to train a child in how he should go, literally, everything you want your children to be; you have to teach them that way. If you want them to speak clear English, it's in your hands. If you want them to be rich, aside from going to school, give them intelligent investment lectures to help them. Training them to have skills is also essential because when education does not bring income, skills will. At these critical stages of their lives, they need you more than ever; please don't be too busy for them. If you don't give them basic training, they will learn anything being thrown at them, and they are forced to decide which is best for them at that young age.

At this stage, they will have critical questions because they have no experience. They are JOT - *Jobs on the training*. They look up to you in actions and direction on where to go. Whatever you don't teach them will be a struggle amongst their peers to get.. And yes, you won't know everything, but being there can solve at least 60% of their problems. They might be trying to articulate some issues you might not notice if you are absent. Please be there. I know they will come out great by God's grace and leading.

Also, parents, each child needs different degrees of attention, love and training according to their personality traits. It was taught that every child should be loved equally in the past, but different types of temperaments do not permit this. And there is a way you can show love without creating envy in their siblings' hearts.

TAKEAWAY NOTES

Children are different; please don't compare them to anyone; their temperament, strengths, and weaknesses are different. No matter how similar they may look, they are still different. Please study them and find out how to treat each child uniquely.

Six

The Person of The Holy Spirit

But the Advocate, the Holy Spirit, whom the Father will send in my name, will teach you all things and will remind you of everything I have said to you- John 14:26

I used to be a very timid child. I was scared of everything, the future, death, losing a family member, the unknown, the dark, scary-looking creatures you'd see in movies. I was scared of everything, you name it! I was afraid to the point of almost being mute. I would be in the car with my family members, and they would not be able to hear my voice. I was so conscious of everything; my body, my complexion, my voice.; Those teenage times did not make it easy; puberty hit me so hard that I had a pronounced figure at age 13. I was dark, I thought I had a big nose, and I had severe allergies which made my eyes red all the time. The high school students made fun of anything outside what was considered normal. I had a tiny voice then because I was shy. This made me conscious of everything, and nothing I did was perfect for me no matter how positively it was spoken of.. This had me constantly depressed.

I gave my life to Christ and received the baptism of the Holy Spirit when I was 15. But I was still ruled by fear, so I remained almost mute.

Everything was the same until I understood the person of the Holy Spirit and His work on this earth. See, when Jesus was on this earth, He was able to go to a place and heal the sick, He was able to give peace and comfort to the woman by the well, and He was able to do many other things. However, He was restricted because He could only be in one place at a time. And that is why He told His disciples that it is for their and our benefit (we who are on earth now until Jesus comes) that He has to leave so that the Holy Spirit will come. See, the Holy Spirit is not limited by time and place. He can be everywhere at the same time. That is the benefit we have as believers.

THE PERSON OF THE HOLY SPIRIT

The Holy Spirit is a person; He has emotions; he can laugh, talk, and get angry as a person with feelings does (Ephesians 4:30). The Holy Spirit dwells in you the moment you give your life to Christ, and you will speak in tongues and heal the sick once you have received His baptism. You can speak to Him and hear Him talk just like you'll do to a friend. But the difference with Him is that He is God and works to help you when you speak to Him.

The Gentleman: The Holy Spirit is a gentleman, and until you involve Him, He won't do anything. He won't interfere. You have to ask Him to help you before He does anything. He does not intrude into your personal affairs without your permission.

The Holy Spirit reveals the mind of the Father: The Holy Spirit is one of the God-Head; His job on earth is to comfort, teach you and bring to your remembrance what Jesus had taught while He was on earth. The Holy Spirit makes us know the mind and will of the Father - God. (1 Corinthians 2:9-12). The Holy Spirit reveals the mind of God as it is only the Spirit that knows what the mind is thinking. Therefore, ask Him about situations that you feel left out or confused about, and I'm sure you will get an answer.

The Holy Spirit will teach you what to do: Have you been in a situation you have never experienced before and do not know what to do, leaving you in confusion that troubles your mind? The Holy Spirit is the answer for you. To curb depressive thoughts, the Holy Spirit knows what you need to curb depressive thoughts. He knows how it will happen. He is beside you; you only need to ask him (Luke 11:12).

The Holy Spirit takes away our anxiety: As an adult, you'll tend to worry and be anxious over things like what you'll eat tomorrow, how to save money, your younger siblings, safety and growth of your children, but the Holy Spirit is there to speak peace into your heart. You can cast all your cares on God, telling the Holy Spirit your worries and letting Him do the worrying for you. 1 Peter 5:6-7. Do not worry, for God, the almighty maker of the universe, is with you. Your mind has to be in constant peace. Therefore anxiety and worrying are not allowed. In the Bible, God asks us not to worry about anything, but in all things, in prayer and supplication with thanksgiving, make your request known to God. I underlined Thanksgiving because not all prayers get answered suddenly, and repeated prayers sometimes bring worry doubt, and negative comments that ruin the prayers, but Thanksgiving brings joy and positive words and is a sign of faith. The Holy Spirit helps you to pray this prayer of thanksgiving.

Depression, fear, anxiety, doubt, and trauma can cause someone to be timid, but the opposite of timidity is boldness, and that only comes from the Holy Spirit (Acts 2:4).

The Holy Spirit helps us carry out the commands of God: The Holy Spirit, the helper, will help you with your walk with God. He will help you overcome those things God has asked you not to do, and to do the specific things He has asked you to do. (2 Timothy 1:14).

The Holy Spirit is for Everyone: God is not selective about who He gives the Holy Spirit. As long as you have given your life to Him, He has given you His Spirit. Acts 15:8-9 tells us of how God knows the heart of men and does not discriminate against who to give the Holy Spirit. The Holy Spirit is beside you today; speak to Him, and tell him how you feel without needing to sound mature, poise or perfect.

He bears witness that we are saved: The Holy Spirit bears witness that we are children of God. Because we have Him, we are sure we are saved and will make heaven- (Ephesians 3:5, Ephesians 4:30).

If you realize you have a weakness from the previous chapters, your dependence on the Holy Spirit will make a huge difference and produce positive results. Remember, the Holy Spirit is a person; although you can't see Him, He speaks, laughs, and has emotions as you do. Do not hesitate to tell Him how you feel and watch Him ease the situation.

I conquered all my fears with the Holy Spirit's help by just explaining to Him how I felt. It was like speaking to an imaginary friend and seeing results. I did not need to be praying to talk to the Holy Spirit. There was no particular time allocated to speak to Him. Whenever and wherever I needed help, I just talked to Him like I was speaking to a friend, and He helped me. A practical thing the Holy Spirit taught me how to do was to cook. I honestly did not watch any videos; He told me some secrets about some ingredients, when to pour them in, and how much to pour.

The Holy Spirit is not selective of who He listens to. All you have to do is speak to Him. It might not make sense, but say it how you feel, and I am confident He will help you.

TAKEAWAY NOTES

The Holy Spirit makes this life's journey easier. Jesus said when He was leaving the earth that the Holy Spirit would teach us all things. I no longer have to be scared because the Holy Spirit leads and guides me in everything. So fear and anxiety are all gone. Why should I worry about tomorrow when the Holy Spirit is already in my tomorrow? God said in His word that we should not worry about anything. He says, "let me worry on your behalf. You live life, let me do the worrying for you" . I can now live each day knowing God already orders my next step.

Epilogue

Jesus was born like a child, and He had to pass through everything we pass through each day. Jesus also had to deal with identity, knowing He was the son of God and standing without a waverly thought. The Holy Spirit and the Father had to confirm it when He was baptized by declaring Him as His beloved son in whom the Father was well pleased. (Matthew 3:17). Even the devil had to also try Him by tempting him with these words as he did to Eve in the garden saying if indeed You are the Son of God, turn these stones into bread. Jesus did not need to convince Himself as Eve did, so He did not turn those stones into bread, showing the devil He knew who He was. (Matthew 4:7). See, the devil has only one target, to know if you know who you are; if you don't or are not sure, then he will deceive you and remove you from your position as he did to Adam and Eve and many others today.. You can't be deceived when you are sure of something. And this is the way the devil works, always trying to see if we know who we are. There are certain things God hates like pride, anger, self-glorification, bitterness, fighting etc. All of these actions show that we are trying too hard to prove to others who we are. For example, with anger, we try to prove that we are the bigger person which can lead to fights and pride. In many of these cases, we are trying to prove that we have more than others. Be sure of your identity in Christ.

And in everything, remember to be you while being guided by the restrictions God's word and the Holy Spirit give you. You are the way you are for a purpose. A speaker once said that you were made for the people 600 years from now, and that's why you seem weird to your generation. Don't make restrictions that are not from God, live out for the nations He has started in you.

You were made for a purpose, don't let fear or the naysayers cripple you. Shine bright, for you are made in His image.

Favour Gaibo is an entrepreneur, a songwriter, a gospel singer, and amongst other things, she is also an advocate for young adults and the author of this life-changing book- Help Me Find My Identity. She is originally from Nigeria but now resides in Canada where she coaches teenagers and young adults about life and mental health.

References

L. Claes et al.
Non-suicidal self-injury in adolescents: Prevalence and associations with identity formation above and beyond depression
Personality and Individual Differences
(2014)

Gary Arthur Thomson. First Writers The Sumerians, Pg. 1, November 1 2011.

Otto Lilienthal. Birdflight as the Basis of Aviation: A contribution towards a system of aviation, compiled from the results of numerous experiments. 1889.

Duncan, George S. "The Birthplace of Man." The Scientific Monthly, vol. 29, no. 4, 1929, pp. 359–.62. JSTOR, http://www.jstor.org/stable/14633. Accessed 12 Jul. 2022. (4 rivers)

Lodhi, Abdulaziz Y. "The language situation in Africa today." Nordic Journal of African Studies 2.1 (1993): 11-11.

www.ingramcontent.com/pod-product-compliance
Lightning Source LLC
Chambersburg PA
CBHW042120100526
44587CB00025B/4129